Barbados Travel Guide

Sightseeing, Hotel, Restaurant & Shopping Highlights

Delia Jenson

Copyright © 2015, Astute Press
All Rights Reserved.

No part of this publication may be reproduced, stored in a retrieval system, or transmitted, in any form or by any means without the prior written permission of the publisher, nor be otherwise circulated in any form of binding or cover other than that in which it is published and without similar condition being imposed on the subsequent purchaser.

If there are any errors or omissions in copyright acknowledgements the publisher will be pleased to insert the appropriate acknowledgement in any subsequent printing of this publication.

Although we have taken all reasonable care in researching this book we make no warranty about the accuracy or completeness of its content and disclaim all liability arising from its use

Table of Contents

Barbados 5
   Culture 6
   Location & Orientation 8
   Climate & When to Visit 9

Sightseeing Highlights 11
   Andromeda Botanic Gardens 11
   Flower Forest 13
   Barbados Museum 14
   Folkstone Marine Park 15
   Harrison's Cave 16
   Nidhe Israel Synagogue & Museum 17
   Careenage 18
   Mount Gay Rum Distillery 19
   National Heroes Square 21
   Morgan Lewis Sugar Windmill 21
   Island Tours 22
   Hiking 23
   Water Adventures 24
   Swimming with Sea Turtles 25
   Zipping 26
   Scooter Rides 26
   Popular Neighborhoods 27

Recommendations for the Budget Traveller 28
   Places To Stay 29
   Places to Eat 31
   Places To Shop 34

Barbados

Known as the Little Britain of the Caribbean, Barbados lies to the northeast of mainland South America. The welcoming locals offer a warm, vibrant ambiance and this "pearl island" provides its visitors with more than just superb sandy beaches and the beautiful waters of the Caribbean Sea.

The island features numerous natural attractions, plenty of colorful festivals and affordable accommodations perfectly suited for the budget traveler.

Compared to other islands lying on the fringes of the Caribbean, Barbados offers a more down-to-earth adventure. That's one of the reasons why it attracts millions of tourists from all over the world and is particularly popular with British and North American visitors.

Culture

Barbados has a rich culture and national heritage both of which are deeply entrenched in the country's modern society. The island has undergone various changes in terms of its political history. Among the first peoples to inhabit the island was the Saladoid-Barrancoid, who were then accompanied by ceramic artists, fishermen as well as farmers.

This first group of immigrants came from the Orinoco Valley in Venezuela circa 350AD. The other significant group that migrated and settled in Barbados was the Arawak who primarily came from Latin America circa 800AD. This second group settled in various locations including Saint Luke's Gully, Chandlers Bay and Stroud Point. The Caribs from Latin America were the third group to arrive on the island, where they quickly became the majority group.

The early settlers claim that the island was in fact known as Ichirouganaim before adopting the name Barbados. The early explorer Pedro Campos who arrived on the island in 1536 initially named the island 'Los Barbados,' meaning the 'bearded ones;' he was referring to the ubiquitous fig trees in the island, which spot long filamentous roots.

The British settled in Barbados in 1627 and after a long anti-slavery struggle, the island finally became independent from the British in 1966. While the country primarily depended on cash crops for a long time, the tourism industry became dominant in the 80s. Today, Barbados is one of the most stable democracies in the region and boats a high literacy too. It is also one of the most popular vacation destinations in the Caribbean.

The local people call themselves Bajan. English is the official language but the locals largely communicate in Bajaan, an English pidgin with Creole influences. Attesting to the rich history of the island, the local language is interspersed with West Africa pidgin, African colloquialism and West Indian idioms.

Barbados is markedly an artistically sophisticated country with music, dance and craft in just about every corner of the island. The musical genre Calypso has its origins from the early inhabitants who arrived as slaves on the island and in the Caribbean at large.

Although this genre was introduced in the country in the seventeenth century, it became better organized in the 1970s. Presently, this music genre is an intricate element of the Barbadian culture. Due to the musical culture inherent in the country, music and art festivals that pour out to the streets are very common.

The warm and genuine hospitality of the people of Barbados is simply memorable. The locals are very welcoming of tourists and they will receive visitors with open arms and frequent embraces. They are quick to lighten up the situation through humorous jokes, dance and music. Tourists are always surprised by the willingness of the locals to show them around and offer assistance.

The society is not deeply divided along social status lines. In fact, it is not uncommon for simple homes to nestle next to palatial houses. Everyone, from the simple beach vendors to the working classes in the major cities, elucidates an air of optimism.

Barbadians are deeply religious but they are equally open-minded and mindful of others. They love festivities and much of daily life is characterized by a sense of celebrating life as well as a humorous disposition. British legacy is still very much a part of the Barbadian experience. Attending church continues to be an important part of the society. Dressing in Sunday bests, (dresses and suits), is an old tradition that persists to date.

Location & Orientation

Barbados is made up of eleven states also known as parishes that can be categorized into four broad regions. These include:

Bridgetown: This is the country's capital city and encompasses the areas around Saint Michael Parish.

Central East region: This is essentially the east coast and covers four parishes including, Saint Andrews, Saint George, Saint Thomas, and Saint Joseph.

Western region: This is the quieter side of the island with the major towns being Speightstown and Holetown. The western region encompasses Saint James, Saint Lucy, and Saint Peter.

Southern region: This is a region popular with tourists lured by the vibrant restaurants and discos and proximity to the Adams International airport. It hosts the parishes of Saint Thomas and Christ Church.

Climate & When to Visit

The weather in this beautiful island is generally sunny and pleasantly warm all throughout the year. The average temperatures during the day range between 78 and 85 Fahrenheit or 29 and 26 degrees centigrade, respectively.

The trade winds, blowing from the northeast make the weather pleasant. Even when it is sunny, the warmth is bearable. The rains usually come in quick showers. It rains mostly in the summer when a refreshing drizzle is always appreciated. The brief rains are followed by bright blue skies, almost immediately. The dry season lasts from January to June.

The island also experiences rainstorms during the hurricane period, which starts in June and runs to October. While the tropical downpour is very heavy, the water rapidly drains into the Sea, leaving the mainland generally dry.

The most popular time to visit the island of Barbados is between December and April when the weather is entirely pleasant. June and October are not favorable for vacation due to the possible hurricanes and rainstorms. However, accommodation costs are likely to be low during this period given that there are not many tourists vacationing in the island.

Sightseeing Highlights

From the lush green landscapes, to the rocky terrains, to the historical monuments, Barbados is an island full of character and inspirational sights. In each activity and in every site visited you will be mesmerized by the sheer beauty and heritage that the island elucidates. Here are some of the places to go and things to do you cannot afford to miss:

Andromeda Botanic Gardens

The Andromeda Gardens are situated on the Atlantic Coast, in St. Joseph Parish.

It is undeniably one of the most picturesque attractions on the Island, opening up to the Tent Bay in Bathsheba. The beautiful gardens propagate the Barbados tradition of gardening. This vast six-acre green space spots colorful flower varieties, orchids, palms as well as cactus plants that cover every inch of the garden to bring out a deeply attractive lush. A clear stream meanders through the lush green plantation; waterfalls and tiny lagoons can be seen everywhere.

The name 'Andromeda' originates from the mythic Greek goddess who is said to have been tied to a rock, just as the house in the middle of this garden and the natural attractions here are. A local horticulturalist, Mrs. Iris Bannochie, began working on the Garden in 1954, when she started planting flower species from all over the world. She later entrusted it to the Barbados National Trust, allowing the locals and tourists to visit the Garden and enjoy the serenity that it offers. In addition to the brightly clustered plantations and flowers that welcome visitors, the café and the gift shop offer a space for relaxing and further exploration of the local culture.

Address: Bathsheba- St Joseph Parish
Contact number: 246/433-9384

Cost: Adults are charged BD$20, while children pay half the price.

Open: The garden is open each day from 9am to 5pm; however, it remains closed on Easter Sunday, Good Friday, Kadooment Day, Christmas Day and Emancipation day. The last time for admission is 4.30pm

Flower Forest

The Flower Forest in the island of Barbados is a strikingly beautiful natural attraction nestled in the Richmond district of St. Joseph Parish. The facility has close proximity to the popular Welchman Gully Hall and the Harrison's Cave. The Flower Forest is a carefully manicured and vast flower landscape hosting a wide array of tropical flowers and plant species.

The bright hues of the *heliconias* are particularly eye-catching and it is tempting to simply stare at the flowers the entire time you are in the Forest. The sights of the green monkey, an indigenous species of the Forest, will also surprise visitors. This is an ideal attraction to visit, for those looking for tranquility and for an intimate experience with nature. The lyrical chirping of the bird species flying across the sky or nesting among the trees only intermittently interrupts the stillness of the forest.

Visitors can tour the Forest on their own but it is possible to book a tour guide to show you around the facility. The guided tours last about forty-five minutes and may present the best option if you do not have adequate time to simply stroll around at your own leisure. Visitors can further indulge in the charms of Barbados at the well-stocked gift shop that sells local souvenirs. Additionally, the snack bar nearby offers scrumptious servings of the flying fish, a popular local dish. The facility is accessible by wheelchair

Address: Highway, 2. Richmond, St. Joseph parish
Phone: 246/433-8152
www.flowerforestbarbados.com

Cost: BD$20 for adults and half price for children

Open: Monday through to Friday from 9am to 5am.

Barbados Museum

The Barbados Museum snuggles quietly on the peripheries of the Garrison Savannah, in St. Michael parish. It is presently located where the historic British military prison was and which was later, in 1930, transformed into the Barbados Museum and Historical Society headquarters. Not only does the building attest to the rich history of the island but also hosts artifacts that symbolize the national heritage, culture and traditions of the Barbadian experience.

The interior of the museum is allows visitors to learn and at the same time enjoy the authentic feeling of being in a place saturated with preserved history and heritage. The Art Festival that takes place in December will also entertain visitors. During the entire period, the museum is awash with local crafts available for viewing and for purchasing. The gift shop and the card collections center offer a wide array of souvenirs, books, prints as well as maps of the island.

Address: St. Ann's Garrison, St Michael
Phone: 246/ 427-0201/
website: www.barbmuse.org.bb

Costs: Adults pay BDS $15 and Children pay BDS $7.50. Rates for group visits are available.

Open: Monday to Saturday from 9am to 5pm and on Sundays from 2pm to 6pm.

Folkstone Marine Park

The Folkstone Marine Park lies next to the graceful St. James Parish Church in Holetown. This scenic facility houses a marine museum that displays underwater species and caters to picnickers looking for quiet escapades. The park spots picnic benches that overlook the expansive Sea. Close by, is a reef created in 1976 after a Greek ship sank off the coast. The naturally formed reef is a popular attraction for visitors, offering incredible visibility and a flurry of brightly colored underwater life for snorkelers and divers.

If you are not very keen about taking an adventure in the waters, marvel at the glorious variety of underwater species through a glass-bottomed canoe tour. One of the major attractions in the Folkstone Park is the museum, hosting marine life displayed in a large aquarium that is certain to amaze both adult and young visitors. It is free to enter the park where visitors can host picnics but a small fee is required to visit the museum.

Address: Highway, 1, Church Point in Holetown- St. James Parish

Phone: 246/425-2871

Cost: 60 cents for museum fee and free for the park

Open: Park is open all throughout and the museum is open from Monday to Saturday from 9am to 5am

Harrison's Cave

The Harrison's Cave is a world-renowned attraction, located in St. Thomas Parish. This majestic cave derived its name from Thomas Harrison, a British settler who owned large strips of the land in the 1700s. In the eighteenth and nineteenth centuries, many explorers had tried, to no avail to gain access to the Harrison's Cave.

The natural entryways made it difficult for anyone to access the cave and to comprehensively explore it. Explorers from Denmark, through their engineering expertise, were finally able to open up the cave's entryways to make it accessible. This magnificent attraction has also had significant renovations, making it safe and feasible to stroll in the area and to view the artefacts on display.

To access the cave, visitors can use the elevator or opt for the adventure of walking through the rugged trails. The highlights of the Cave are the hanging and grounded salt pillars protruding in the caves. The Cave also spots natural-forming waterfalls that run down to crystal clear lagoons.

Address: Highway, 2 Welchman Hall- St. Thomas parish
Phone: 246/417-3700/
website: www.harrisonscave.com

Cost: BD $ 30 for adults and half price for children

Open: Daily from 8.30 am to 4.30 pm and the last time for admission is at 3.45pm

Nidhe Israel Synagogue & Museum

The Nidhe Israel Synagogue is the oldest religious site not just in the island of Barbados but also in the Western hemisphere. The synagogue stands on Synagogue Lane in Bridgetown. This is a major attraction for visitors looking to learn about the Jewish heritage and history in the island. The Jewish settlers in Barbados played a significant role in establishing the sugar industry, which was for a long time the island's mainstay. Because of the successful sugar industry, the island was known as the Jewel in The Crown.

The Nidhe Israel Synagogue offers an inspired perspective and celebration of the Jewish culture. Importantly, the Synagogue is a unique attraction that offers a different type of Mikvah - a complete immersion.

The existing synagogue was reconstructed after the original one was destroyed by hurricanes in 1831. The newly built synagogue is a stunning building espousing Jewish, Barbadian and Gothic architectural influences. The early Jews who inhabited this area offered the Bridgetown community a gift in form of the Montefiore Fountain located at the center of the synagogue and the public library.

Address: Synagogue Lane, Bridgetown,
Phone: 246/436-6869

Open: Monday to Friday from 9am to 4pm; weekend visits can be reserved

Costs: Adults are charged BD $25 and children pay BD $12; it is free for children under the age of five years.

Careenage

Located in the heart of the island of Barbados, the Careenage is one of the most visited attractions by both tourists and locals. The Careenage gained its popularity in 1628 following the entry of the British settlers in the country.

There was not much in the region at the time except for a wooden bridge over the waters. It is claimed that one of the first groups to settle in the island, the Arawaks, created the bridge. When the British settlers came across the bridge, they began to refer to the area as the Indian Bridge. The British replaced this old bridge with another one and the area adopted the name Saint Michael and later the Bridgetown.

The major highlights of the Careenage are the two bridges, the Chamberlain Bridge and the Charles Dancun O'Neal Bridge. The latter extends throughout the river into the bus terminus at Fairchild Street. The Chamberlain Bridge extends from the Trafalgar Square to the opposite bank. The boardwalk close to the Careenage offers an exciting place to take an evening walk, to watch as the boats, yachts and catamarans dock, or simply to enjoy the expansive vista of the horizon that lies ahead. If you are looking to get away from the flurry of the city, the Careenage will be a great choice.

Address: Bridgetown, St. Michael

Mount Gay Rum Distillery

The Mount Gay Rum Distillery is one of the oldest and 'must visit' attractions that take you back to the distilling history of this Caribbean island. The day tour through this ancient distillery allows visitors to learn the secrets about the manufacturing of some of the country's finest golden rum. This distillery is more than 300 years old but still produces some of the best rum the world has ever known.

It is located off Brandons beaches in St. Michael parish. The distillery nestles unassumingly in the lush tropical vegetation and churns out the seductive aroma of rum that is simply memorable to those who visit. The Distillery also houses a Museum, which serves as keeper of its history.

Visitors will certainly want to explore the Bajan Rum Shop with its authentic and diversified ingredients that are used to manufacture the tantalizing drinks. The cocktail tour to the Mount Gay Bar is also one to look forward to; guests get to have a laugh and merry as they compete to make the best cocktails against the very experienced Bajan bartenders. There are prizes to be won for the most innovative cocktail!

In addition to the flavorful drinks, guests can enjoy a scrumptious meal of traditional foods alongside a refreshing glass of Barbadian rum cocktail. After lunch, be sure to take a stroll to the gift shop where you can marvel at the eccentric paraphernalia relating to Mount Gay Rum. This is the ideal location to grab a local souvenir and to carry with you a bottle of Bajan rum at affordable prices. Guests are required to make early reservations for lunch and the cocktail tour.

Address: Spring Garden Highway,
Brandons- St. Michael parish
Phone: 246/425-8757
website: www.mountgayrum.com

Cost: The forty-five minute tour is US $7 and free for children; the lunch tour is US $50 and half price for children while the cocktail tour is $35.

Open: Monday to Friday from 9am to 5pm; the first tour to the distillery starts at 9.30am while the last tour starts at 2.30pm.

National Heroes Square

The National Heroes Square was initially known as Trafalgar square. This national site is located in the capital Bridgetown and flanks a majestic statue of Lord Nelson, who visited the island in 1805. The statute was put up to celebrate Britain's victory in the Trafalgar battles. This open place became known as the National Heroes Square, in 1999.

This vast square attracts visitors looking to take pictures of the national heritage sites and just to have a feel of the Barbadian city life. Other nearby attractions include the Dolphin Fountain and the War Memorial, which honor Barbadians who fought in the two world wars. While on vacation in the island be sure to visit the National Heroes Square to meet people in the city and to check out the nearby attractions.

Morgan Lewis Sugar Windmill

The Morgan Lewis Mill is among the largest and ancient mills in the island of Barbados and still maintains some of its old glory. The mill was instrumental in running the sugar industry in the Island and aided in the production of the world-renowned Barbadian sugar. Visitors fascinated by history and ancient development will gasp at the magnificent photographs displaying the historic days when sugar was the mainstay of the country's economy and society.

The mill snuggles in a bucolic hillside in the stunning northeast cost. Nearby attractions, include the beach neighborhood of Bathsheba and the Wildlife Reserve. Vendors selling ice creams and refreshing tropical drinks are scattered throughout the area. Vigorous efforts to conserve the mill have ensured that it remains one of the top cultural attractions in the island.

Address: South East, Cherry Tree Hill, Morgan Lewis- St. Andrews parish
Phone: 246/422-7429

Open: from Monday to Friday from 9 am to 5pm

Costs: Adults are charged BD $10 while children pay half the price.

Island Tours

Visitors looking to explore different parts of the island will like the adventurous and fun-filled island tours. The tours offer access to the island's magnificent landscapes ranging from the rugged and unexplored beaches of the east coast to the breathtaking natural attractions of the south coast. The island tours will take you to the highest peak in Barbados, the Mount Hilaby and then bring you down to the Chalky Mount where you can meet the locals as they undertake their artwork. As you head to the heart of the island, be sure to stop by the Welchman Hall Gully, a natural sanctuary that will impress you with its exotic lush vegetation.

Take a trip to the renowned Harrison's Cave that lies in the underground trails. There are many options to choose from; you can hire a scooter, jump on a bike or hike a bus that takes you across the island as you discover its natural wonders, as well as the beauty and charm of the island.

Hiking

If you thought that the tropical island of Barbados only offers turquoise waters and soft sandy beaches, think again. The island offers plenty of opportunity for the more adventurous traveller looking to break a sweat. The natural terrain and beaten tracks offer an ideal landscape for hiking. The hiking trips take guests to bucolic villages inland; they thrust you to the heart of vast mazes of sugar cane fields and land you in the thick of the tropical rainforests.

Hikers are constantly amazed by the natural charm and diversity exhibited by the island's terrain. Missing a hike would certainly be missing out on the natural adventures underlying the island of Barbados, just waiting to be explored. If you are looking for a resourceful way to spend your weekend afternoons while on the island, the Barbados National Trust Hike is an excellent option. The hikes start at various points and take place on Sundays starting from 6am to 3.30pm.

Guests can choose various hiking categories depending on the type of experience one is looking for. The 'Stop-n-Stare' hikes cover about 6 miles of an educative, guided tour that mixes adventure with historical education. The 'Here-n-here' hike covers an estimated 10 miles and is more of a fast walk than a stroll. Lastly, hikers can participate in the intense 'Grin-n-Bare' tour that covers up to 14 miles. More adventure awaits hikers with the moonlight hikes that kick off at 5.30pm. It is advisable to come with a torch for this evening hike.

Water Adventures

The water adventures in Barbados are endless. While the waters of the west coast may encourage calmness, they also offer an arena of utter enjoyment for their guests. The Seafari, for example, is one of the most enthralling water-based activities on the island. If you are looking for a thrill, jump on board the aptly named Thriller Powerboats and enjoy the adrenalin rush as the boat blasts its way through the waves. A trained and experienced captain accompanied by his crew navigates the powerboat, which can accommodate up to 35 people.

Alternatively, explore the sea on board the Atlantis Submarines, which plunges you into the breathtaking depths of the vast Caribbean Sea. Your underwater tour will expose you to ancient shipwrecks, multicoloured sea species as well as stunning coral reefs. The submarine adventure is especially popular with families but everyone will love the underwater exploration. An experienced pilot will guide you through the voyage.

The underwater tours last up to two and a half hours. Guests aged 17 years and above pay, BD $208 inclusive of drinks while those below 7 years are charged BD $104.

Other water activities that await you include diving, snorkelling, wind surfing, and skiing. Be sure to enjoy the waters of Barbados before your vacation is over.

Swimming with Sea Turtles

Barbados is home to exotic turtle species including the leatherback and hawksbill. The turtles are commonly seen meandering on the shores of the west coast where they feed and nest. The calm waters of the west coast enable guests to swim alongside the turtles. This is an experience that is unique to this part of the Caribbean.

Both adults and younger guests will be thrilled to swim side-by-side with the island's marine life. The Barbados Sea Turtle Project is an initiative that seeks to protect sea turtles in the island and preserve the delicate ecosystem in which the turtles are part of. Reserve your swimming with the turtles adventures with one of the many cruise companies or catamaran companies on the island. Some well-known companies include Barbados Blue, and Rubaiyat Catamaran Cruises.

Zipping

Zipping offers an opportunity to enjoy a birds-eye view of the lush forests of the island while experiencing the rush that comes with sliding down a zip line. Zipping operators such as the Ariel Trek offer tours that cover eight challenging levels. The experienced tour guides are a great source of information for both the technique of zipping and the ecology below.

The zipping tours are suitable for the adventurous as well as those who are looking to do something different while vacationing on the island. Zippers will enjoy gasp-inducing scenery of the island from up above; you will be able to spot landscapes, expansive beaches and bays, and the intensity of the blue waters of the Sea will become even more apparent. After the zipping excursion, take a walk around the jungle or head back to the main base for a revitalizing drink before heading back to your hotel.

Scooter Rides

Nothing beats the feeling of navigating the Barbadian landscape on your own scooter. Make your way through the mud, sand, rock and vegetation while exploring the magnificent wonders the island has to offer. Guests looking for a "messy" excursion cannot afford to miss a scooter ride. You will have numerous photo opportunities. Stop by a shady coconut palm tree under which the locals will serve you a refreshing tropical drink to boost your energy as you proceed on with your scooter tour.

Popular Neighborhoods

As you explore the wonders of this enthralling island, remember to have a look at some of the neighborhoods and the activities going on there.

St. Joseph: Bathsheba, lying along the east coast of Barbados offers some of the most impressive vistas. A jagged coastline laced with lush plantations characterizes the area. This neighborhood is well known for surfing and hosts the annual Caribbean Surfing Championships held at the central beach place in Bathsheba. The accommodation here is simple and affordable for the budget traveller.

St. Lucy: The most popular neighborhood here is North Point. In addition to hosting one of the functioning lighthouses in the country, it also offers amazing vistas of the Sea. On your way to the Animal Flower Cave, drop by the North Point and take part (or just watch!) in some intense high-wave surfing.

Christchurch: In the island's south coast lays St Lawrence Gap, a strip alive with dancing and festivities. Wonderful restaurants and bars will also beckon. The Dove beach is an ideal hangout offering numerous water activities. On your way back from the Oistins fishing dock, end your excursion swaying to the harmonic beats of Bajan music in the St. Lawrence Gap neighborhood.

Recommendations for the Budget Traveller

Barbados offers a wide range of comfortable and affordable accommodation, fantastic places to eat and dine out, as well as endless options for duty free and inexpensive shopping. Indulge in an endless array of exotic cuisines and still have enough for your shopping spree.

Places To Stay

Rio Guesthouse: The Rio Guesthouse is a popular, cozy accommodation located in the vibrant entertainment strip of St. Lawrence Gap. The guesthouse is particularly attractive due to its prime location and its proximity to restaurants, bars and department stores. It is also less than 10 minutes walk to the beach.

The open terrace that flanks the main unit is great for socializing with other guests. For a budget hotel, the rooms are delicately looked after and pleasant to stay in. The staff and the hosts are warm-natured, giving the Rio Guesthouse a friendly ambiance. This is an excellent option for visitors who are looking for a small but vibrant place to unwind.

Address: Paradise Village, St Lawrence Gap, Bridgetown
Phone: +1 246 428 1546
Website: http://www.rioguesthouse.hostel.com/

Peach & Quiet Hotel: This snuggly little hotel will offer a relaxing and memorable holiday experience. It is located in a stunning setting, hidden away on the southern coast of Barbados. If you are looking to unwind and get away from it all at an affordable rate then this may be the choice for you. You can spend as little as $800 for a double room for a week-long stay – and are inclusive of meals. The food is deliciously made and is served at the elegant courtyard in the hotel. In addition to offering neatly decorated rooms, the hosts are very cordial, and knowledgeable about the island. The spacious rooms have either a garden view, a view of the ocean or of the stylish swimming pool.

Address: Inch Marlow Main Road,
Inch Marlow, Christchurch
Phone: 246 428 5682
Website: www.peachandquiet.com

Desert Rose: The aptly named Desert Rose is a gem, nestled in a tranquil environment that allows you to simply wind down at your own pace. The main house features four bedrooms, three showers, a living space and a furnished kitchen, perfect for guests looking for a self-catering getaway. In addition to the tranquility offered at the Desert Rose hotel, you will enjoy the graciousness demonstrated by the hosts Heidrun and Ann as well as Pat, the housekeeper. The hotel is located in the lively neighborhood of St. Lawrence Gap and the sandy Dover beach is just 5 minutes' walk away.

Address: Dover, St Lawrence, Christchurch
Phone: 246 428 4760

Legend Garden Condos: This is an impressive property with exceptional hosts, Delia and Bird. The rooms are filled with the refreshing tropical breeze and each room has its unique décor, specially designed by Delia. The units feature a well-equipped kitchen in the outdoors, ideal for families or groups looking to self-cater during their vacation. The hotel features an elegant swimming pool from where you can have a spectacular view of monkeys agilely hopping from one tree to another. It is a short strolling distance to the Mullins and Gibbes Beaches; Mullins beach bustles with activity while Gibbes offers a more serene experience if you are looking to have a quiet time at the beach.

Address: Mullins Bay, St. Peter
Phone: 246 422 8369
E-mail: legendcondos@sunbeach.net
website: www.legendcondos.com

All Seasons Resort-Europa: Cuddled in the Sunset Crest area of St James parish, the All Seasons Resort-Europa offers serenity for guests looking for a place to escape the hustle and bustle of your vacation. The magnificent Paynes Bay and Beach awaits you while Just Grillin' is a great place to spend the afternoon or evenings enjoying its scrumptious delicacies. Rooms are adequately spacious, delicately manicured and the beddings are enticingly crisp. Some rooms overlook the lush green gardens while others open up to the blue waters of the pool.

Address: Palm Avenue, Sunset Crest, St. James
Email: stay@allseasonsresort.bb
Phone: +1-246-432-5046
Website: http://www.allseasonsresort.bb/

Places to Eat

Barbeque Barn: This is an excellent choice and offers affordable prices for delightfully made food. The Barn allows you to take pleasure in casual dining which creates a memorable ambience.

This restaurant is particularly suited for those looking to eat healthy as it serves freshly made salads appetizingly displayed at the elegant salad buffet. Enjoy mouthwatering and perfectly broiled choice steaks, fish fillets and burgers with any choice of side meal, all at a reasonable price.

Cassareep Cafe on the Beach: Offers a beautiful setting, as it cradles amidst the trees of the island. Cassareep is the perfect beach café/ restaurant with stunning views of the sea, delightful delicacies and refreshing cocktails. The shaded decks open up to the majestic Speightstown pier.

The service here is impressive, and guest are largely treated to cuisines with Indian influences including the Pad Thais as well as nutty and tangy PuriRotti, just to mention a few. Cassareep is an enviable spot for a casual lunch or dinner. What makes this café/restaurant so attractive and affordable for the budget traveler is that it offers specials each day, making the mouthwatering foods a complete bargain. The staff offers the unmistakable charm that is characteristic of Bajans.

Address: Cassareep Cafe, Seaside Courts,
Speightstown - St Peter
Phone: 246 422 3573
Website: http://www.cassareep.com/

Fisherman's Pub: If you are looking for a truly local Bajan experience, then the Fisherman's Pub offers an ambience that will suit you.

This is an outdoors restaurant cradled at the beachfronts of Speights town. A great budget choice, it offers some of the most authentic and affordable local cuisines. For just $10, you can enjoy generous servings of finger-licking delicacies including fried plantains, freshly made salads, curried chicken, pork, beef and the popular flying fish, fried to perfection. Wednesday night is Calypso night when you can sway to the harmonious beats while enjoying the variety of barbeques on offer.

Address: Queen Street,
Speightstown - St. Peter
Phone: 246-422-2703
Email: pub@caribsurf.com
Website: http://www.fishermanpub.com/

Bombas: This is a small bar and restaurant lying by the beach and flanked by wooden decks. It lies at the heart of one of the most scenic beaches on the island of Barbados, the Paynes Bay and Beach. Gay, a chef from Scotland and Wayne, a local of Barbados, skillfully operate Bombas. This is an excellent choice if you are looking for al fresco dining. Some of the impressive mouthwatering specials include tangy pasta sauces, well thought-out vegetarian dishes that are set to entice ardent 'carnivores', as well as South East Asian sauces and curries. The menu also features a tantalizing offer of chicken and fish-based cuisines and the signature 'Bombaburger.'

Address: Turtle Bay, North Mullins-St. Peter
Phone: 246 432 5664
Email: wayne@bombasbeachbar.net
Website: http://bombasbeachbar.net/

Café Sol Mexican Grill: You can never go wrong with Mexican cuisine and Café Sol Mexican Grill offers you exactly that authentic Mexican experience. This little gem, tacked in the interiors of St. Lawrence Gap offers affordable, scrumptious food for excellent value. Indulge in the Mojito chicken or choose the flame grilled burgers and the sophisticated and delicately made cocktails. You will love happy hour, which lasts from 5pm to 7pm for the first session and the second happy hour comes in the late evenings, accompanying the dance and festivity, typical of Barbados.
Address: St. Lawrence Gap – Christchurch
Phone: 246-420 7655
Website: http://www.cafesolbarbados.com/

Places To Shop

Swan Street: Barbados is always bustling with vendors selling their wares along the streets and the city hosts large shopping malls, department stores and duty free shopping. The Swan Street is fantastic for purchasing local crafts, prints, jewelry as well as grocery.

Broad Street: Board Street features a maze of small streets and pathways awash with affordable wares of all types. You can buy a customized pair of leather shoes in just a couple of minutes; the immensely skilled shoe vendors can shape and design a pair of shoe for you as you watch. Other affordable places in Bridgetown to do your shopping include the Cave Shepherd, which hosts numerous duty free stalls.

Oistins: Oistins offers a Bajan feel with many stalls that display and sell local crafts. The market is typically colorful with the handmade wears that are reasonably priced. You can walk away with small pearls of jewelry or with a large sized Bajan-crafted statue all from the same market. Friday night is fish night and Oistins comes to life with an ecstatic and celebrative atmosphere as locals vend fresh and grilled fish. The Oistin Fish Fry Friday is the ideal time to purchase some of the island's best fishes, at inexpensive prices.

Pelican Crafts Centre: Located along Harbor Road, Pelican Craft Center spots various craft stores each offering unrivaled charm especially for the tourist. Some tourists claim that the shops here are unnecessarily overpriced. However, it is possible to find reasonably priced and authentically Bajan handmade items that will continue to epitomize your experience on the island, long after your vacation is over.

Address: Princess Alice Highway,
Bridgetown - St Michael
Phone: 246-426 0765

Highland Pottery: This is an artists' hub where local curators produce meticulously crafted pottery, leatherworks and paintings. Located in St. Andrews Parish, and on the fringes of Chalky Mountain, Highland Pottery offers you the opportunity to shop for local handmade pots, vases, mugs, plates as well as jewelry. The local artists create their multi-colored wares from locally sourced raw material. Do not hesitate to indulge in Bajan artwork; it will be worth it for the memories it will invoke.

Address: Chalky Mountain, St. Andrew
Phone: 246-422-9818

Printed in Great Britain
by Amazon